MICHAE

The
Wicklow
Way

from Marley to Glenmalure

A Walking Guide

GILL AND MACMILLAN

Published in Ireland by
Gill and Macmillan Ltd
Goldenbridge
Dublin 8
with associated companies in
Auckland, Delhi, Gaborone, Hamburg, Harare, Hong Kong,
Johannesburg, Kuala Lumpur, Lagos, London, Manzini,
Melbourne, Mexico City, Nairobi, New York, Singapore,
Tokyo
© Michael Fewer 1988
Cover photo by Bill Doyle
Print origination by Graphic Plan, Dublin 1
Printed in Hong Kong

British Library of Congress Cataloguing in Publication Data

Fewer, Michael
   The Wicklow way: a walking guide.
   1. Wicklow (County) — Description and
   travel — Guide-books
   I. Title
   796.5′1′094184   DA990.W6

   ISBN 0-7171-1550-X

Maps in this book are based on the
Ordnance Survey by permission of the
Government (Permit No. 4854).

CONTENTS

The approximate mileage and the type of terrain to be expected are given with each section.

Key to Terrain Types

Tarmacadam road or track	A
Gravel road or track	B
Mountain track	C
Cross country (no formal track)	D
Steep ascents or descents	E

INTRODUCTION

Until the establishment of the Wicklow Way in 1980, the remoter parts of the Dublin and Wicklow Mountains were enjoyed only by a fortunate few serious hill walkers and mountainclimbers; today this magnificent walking route laid out by J. B. Malone has opened up the treasure chest of the uplands to even the casual stroller. There is something here for everyone, including dramatic secenery, wildlife of all kinds and splendid exercise in the freshest of air.

This guide is intended primarily for strollers and family groups and covers the most frequented and accessible part of the Wicklow Way, from Marley to Glenmalure.

As well as describing the Way in sections of varying length, the guide indicates a number of circuits that can be made from points along the route and some alternative sections to the main Way. While some trekking over open and sometimes steep hillsides is involved, most of the routes described are over public or forestry roads and tracks and there are no sections that reasonably fit adults and children couldn't handle in good conditions. The Contents page includes information on distances and type of terrain involved in the different sections described in the guide.

The Wicklow Way is indicated along the route by timber posts with a yellow arrow pointing the way, so if you keep a keen eye out for turning points you should not go far astray. While simple maps are included to show the immediate surroundings to the Way and the Alternative routes and Circuits described, it is recommended that more detailed information such as the Ordnance Survey Wicklow Way Map is carried also, particularly for the longer walks and walks in remote areas. The maps detailing the route are at a scale of 1:50,000, or 1 inch equals four-fifths of a mile. Each map overlaps its neighbours to help continuity and the top of the map is towards north.

Occasionally I have found signposts missing at junctions, tracks which have been obliterated by the debris of harvested sections of forestry, and fords or bridges over streams swept away by storms. While these kinds of problems can add an

1

element of challenge to a mountain walk, be prudent if you encounter them and if in doubt, turn back.

While a stroll through Marley Park needs little preparation, the further south you go on the Wicklow Way the more you should consider the suitability of your clothing and what you need to bring with you. Suitable footwear is extremely important; even in summertime many places in the mountains remain quite wet and muddy. A small knapsack is useful for carrying waterproofs and additional warm clothing, and no matter how short the walk, a packed snack is always welcome. Even some chocolate or fruit helps to inject a new surge of energy when spirits are flagging! A compass can be handy, particularly in the remote areas, used in conjunction with an Ordnance Map. A walking stick makes hill walking considerably easier and if approached by an unfriendly dog, you usually only have to raise it in warning to be rid of him. A whistle and a torch will take up very little room in your knapsack, but could be essential if an emergency arises.

While much of the Wicklow Way is close to public roads and houses, some areas like Djouce and Mullacor are quite remote where a minor injury like a sprained ankle can cause major problems. Always ensure there are enough 'bodies' in your group to deal with such eventualities. Weather conditions in the mountains can change rapidly and become very severe, so don't attempt remoter sections without some experience, don't set out if the forecast is bad, keep an eye on the weather during your walk and always bring suitable clothing to deal with wind, wet and cold.

The additional routes (Circuits and Alternatives) in this guide are over lands where walkers are not currently forbidden to trespass; however, ownership and attitudes can change, so if in doubt, ask permission.

Finally, some important do's and don'ts regarding mountain walking:

Always let someone know where you are going and what time to expect you back.

Start modestly if you have little previous experience and build up to the longer walks.

Don't go alone into the mountains.

Don't depart from marked paths or forest roads if the weather deteriorates.

2

Don't attempt what you think is a short cut unless you are an experienced hill walker.

Don't damage fences, walls or gates.

Don't bring a dog, unless he is on a lead all of the time.

Don't leave litter behind you and don't light a fire within one mile of any state forest.

Sparrow-hawk

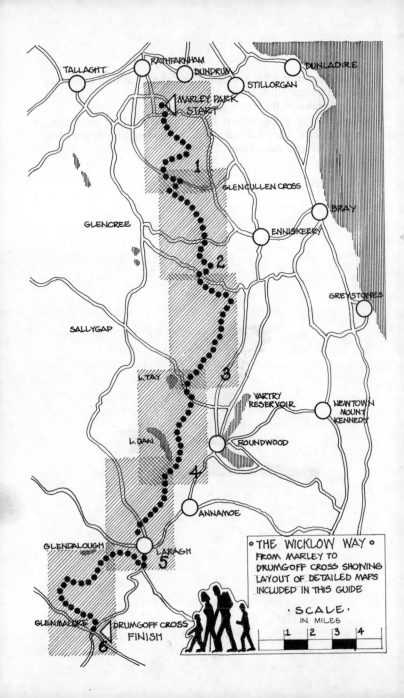

TALLAGHT

RATHFARNHAM
DUNDRUM

DUNLAOIRE
STILLORGAN

MARLEY PARK
START

1

GLENCULLEN CROSS

GLENCREE

BRAY

ENNISKERRY

2

GREYSTONES

SALLYGAP

3

L.TAY

VARTRY
RESERVOIR

NEWTOWN
MOUNT
KENNEDY

L.DAN

ROUNDWOOD

4

ANNAMOE

GLENDALOUGH

LARAGH
5

GLENMALURE

DRUMGOFF CROSS
FINISH
6

° THE WICKLOW WAY °
FROM MARLEY TO
DRUMGOFF CROSS SHOWING
LAYOUT OF DETAILED MAPS
INCLUDED IN THIS GUIDE

· SCALE ·
IN MILES

1   2   3   4

KEY TO DETAILED MAPS

WICKLOW WAY ROUTE	●●●●●●●●●●●
ALTERNATIVE ROUTES & CIRCUITS	○○○○○○○○○○○
PUBLIC ROADS	
FOREST	
CONTOURS	700 600
RIVERS	
CAR PARKS	ⓟ
MOUNTAIN PEAKS	1840 ▲

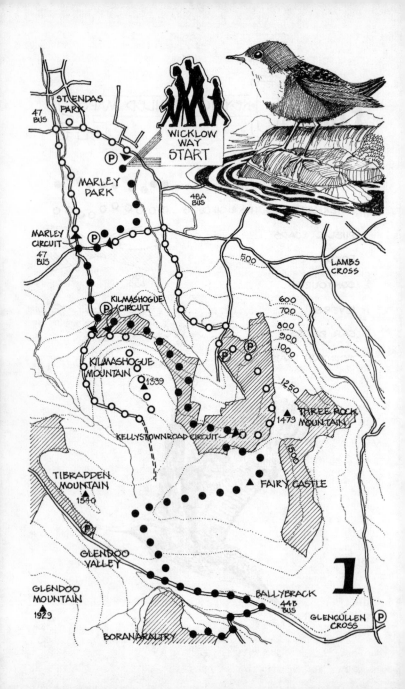

MARLEY PARK
to
KILMASHOGUE WOOD

The Wicklow Way begins easily, even seductively, on well-paved level surfaces, through the parkland of one of Ireland's finest public amenities, Marley Park. Marley covers over two hundred acres and provides within its boundaries a variety of walks, a nine hole golf course, tennis courts, playing fields, a fabulous adventure playground and a miniature railway.

The Wicklow Way route through the park combines open spaces, narrow forest tracks, streams and lakes with many little waterfalls and fairy-tale bridges. Pieces of modern fun sculpture scattered throughout the woodland excite and intrigue children of all ages.

Marley House was built around 1794 by one of the La Touche family, who ran a successful banking house at Castle Street in Dublin. The magnificent plastered ceiling of their original bank was removed piece by piece in 1946 and re-assembled in the Bank of Ireland in College Green where it can be seen today. Apart from counting four Members of Parliament amongst their number, the La Touches were connected by marriage to Henry Grattan and at one time owned such properties as Luggala Lodge in Co. Wicklow and four houses in St Stephen's Green, in addition to houses at Ely Place and Merrion Square.

At the same time as the house at Marley was built, the demesne containing 400 acres was laid out and extensively landscaped. More than 300 varieties of trees and shrubs were planted and the Little Dargle River was harnessed into a series of waterfalls and lakes. Extensive glasshouses were erected which at the time of Samuel Lewis's visit in the 1830s were 'stocked with a large selection of native and exotic plants'. The La Touches' farming, like their other business ventures, was highly successful, particularly in the cultivation and production of many acres of potatoes for export to England.

The tall trees, thick undergrowth, lakes and streams of the park make a successful habitat for birds and small mammals and I have found that if you set out on the Wicklow Way early, before the park becomes too populated, you have a good chance of seeing the shyer ones.

The squirrel is probably the most charming of our four-footed animals and one of the few it is possible to catch sight of during the day.

Ireland has two species of squirrel, the red squirrel which has been here since the last Ice Age and the grey, which was introduced from America in the last century. The red squirrel can be seen in Marley; he's about fifteen inches long in all, including seven inches of bushy red tail and unlike the grey, has marked tufts of fur on his ears.

There are a number of locations where squirrels make their nests or drays in Marley; one of the Park Attendants may be able to direct you to one. The dray is constructed in the fork of a tree of twigs and bark and is lined with soft mosses and grass.

Red squirrels enjoy feeding on acorns, hazelnuts and berries, but their favourite meal is oil-rich pine seeds and when I suspect they may be present in a wood I look for a scattering of stripped pine cones beneath the trees. Squirrels are very shy and noise and movement are danger signals for them, but if you move quietly and 'freeze' as soon as you spot one, you may be able to observe the animal foraging and feeding.

You are never far from water on the Wicklow Way route through Marley and this presents an opportunity to see a variety of waterbirds at close quarters. While the mallard and the shyer moorhen can be easily observed, careful watching can reward you with a sighting of the dipper. The dipper is a distant cousin of the wren though a lot bigger and has a white bib; often it is this bib that catches the eye when seeking him out. If you are lucky, you may see this unusual bird actually 'flying' under water in search of food.

The Wicklow Way exits Marley opposite the gates of St Columba's College, a co-educational boarding school. Once considered the Eton of Ireland, up to some years ago boys were obliged to wear straw hats or bowlers on 'exeats' or outings. When a fire destroyed some of the buildings in 1896, boys escaped from the dormitories using sheets as ropes. The Fire Brigade took three hours to get to the fire, delayed because they had to obtain the permission of the Lord Mayor to leave the city!

The red squirrel

The road here is said to be haunted; in penal times a man was summarily executed for carrying a priest in his cart to celebrate Christmas Mass nearby. Every seventh Christmas Eve he is said to return, complete with horse and cart but minus head, to finish the journey.... At the junction of Tibradden Road you can return to the Wicklow Way starting point by continuing down Whitechurch Road (see Marley Circuit below.)

Near the corner of Kilmashogue Lane, look out for a Saorstat Éireann postbox, somewhat of a rarity because relatively few were made. I have heard of examples of this type of postbox being stolen to be sold to foreign collectors! Turning into Kilmashogue Lane, the road crosses a stream and begins to ascend.

The ruins on the right are the remains of the old Kilmashogue school, and Doolan's Woollen Mill, one of the many successful mills which took advantage of the fast flowing river in this area up to the advent of steam. The hill gets quite steep before reaching Kilmashogue Wood where the Wicklow Way turns left onto a forest road. A pleasant little stepped pathway leads from the car park here uphill for rather more than sixty yards to a clearing where you will find a group of megalithic tombs, discovered in 1950, the earliest of which was constructed nearly 4,000 years ago. The original Stone Age burial place was vandalised by Bronze Age people about 3,000 years ago, who dismantled the first tomb to provide stones to build their own chamber! When excavated, the various structures were found to contain considerable quantities of cremated bone, and some finely decorated clay pots. For a circuit of the mountain, see Kilmashogue Circuit, page 14.

MARLEY CIRCUIT

To complete a round trip of under three miles, leave the Wicklow Way route at Tibradden Road to carry on down Whitechurch Road. On the right is New Whitechurch, an elegant example of nineteenth-century Gothic designed by Semple and built about 1825. See if you can spot a large granite slab opposite the church on the roadside, with a socket in it that used to hold a Celtic High Cross. Water lodging in the socket is said to have the power to cure warts!

Further on is the Moravian Cemetery; the Moravians founded the first Independant Protestant Church in 1467, in what is now Czechoslovakia, but were scattered throughout Europe by religious persecution in the seventeenth century. They came to Dublin about 1750, and within a few years had built eighteen chapels in Ireland. It was rumoured that Moravians were buried either sitting or standing; while this is unlikely it is true that women are buried on one side of the graveyard and men on the other.

To the left before the roundabout is the old Whitechurch, dating from the sixteenth century but built over the ruins of an even older establishment. Fixed to the gable of the ruin are two early Christian graveslabs, one with a carved cross which must have weathered nearly a thousand years. There are many eighteenth- and nineteenth-century tombstones with fascinating inscriptions, including one with a carved crucifixion design which includes all the paraphernalia of Calvary including a hammer, nails, ladder, spear, a sponge on a stick and a lash.

Before returning to the main road, take a look into the little private cemetery of the Harty and Porter families beside the church boundary. One of the two doctors buried here is said to have been physician to Queen Victoria.

At the traffic lights, cross the road and enter St Enda's Park. Near the gate is an obelisk erected by a former owner, a Major Doyne, to his horse, which carried him safely through the Battle of Waterloo!

Here at St Enda's Padraig Pearse ran his Irish school for the last six years of his life; the house is now an interesting museum, well worth a visit. Our route however exits the park in the south east corner near a ruined folly called Emmet's Fort, where Robert Emmet is said to have met often with Sarah Curran, who lived just across the road.

The entrance to Marley is now a short distance away, past the Eden Lounge Bar.

New Whitechurch

KILMASHOGUE WOOD
to
GLENDOO VALLEY

Kilmashogue Mountain is the closest spur of the Dublin range to the city and its rather flat summit reaches 1,339 ft above sea level. The remains of the little church founded by St Mashogue are said to have existed near here up to the mid nineteenth century, but their whereabouts are no longer known. A beautifully carved ninth-century cross slab from the church is now located in the chapel of St Columba's College. A circuit of Kilmashogue mountain, starting and ending at the car park, is described on page 14.

Although the forestry track here is long and enclosed by trees, it need not be a boring section for children; there are plenty of 'discoveries' worth looking out for. In places the bank along the side of the road can be seen to contain large boulders of granite that are in the last stages of decay. Granite is the most common rock in the Dublin and Wicklow Mountains and is made up of three minerals, mica, feldspar and quartz. The mix was formed deep in the earth's crust some 400 million years ago and is now exposed on the surface because the original covering layers have been weathered away. The rock can be crumbled between the fingers, demonstrating clearly the concept of erosion, and how entire mountain ranges can disappear in time due to the action of the weather. The track here is bright with individual crystals of shiny mica weathered out from the granite. Children can compete in looking for the biggest flakes and when the layers are peeled apart it can be seen that the material is actually transparent; in fact mica was used in some countries for windows before the advent of glass.

Although there are some gaps in the forest giving glimpses of Stackstown and Ticknock, the first real panorama of the Dublin area comes into view when the Wicklow Way abruptly leaves the forestry road and ascends steeply to the right. To return to Marley via Kellystown Road, continue to follow the forestry road here, see Kellystown Road Circuit (on page 15).

13

As the Wicklow Way route levels out and emerges from the southern edge of the forest, the 1,500 feet contour is passed. In clear weather the serrated line of the Mourne Mountains can be seen on the northern horizon ending in the bulk of Slieve Gullion, and I have frequently seen the mountains of Snowdonia more than seventy miles away on the eastern horizon. All the landmarks of the city are visible from here; see how many you can identify.

To the north east now is Three Rock Mountain, which takes its name from the curiously shaped granite tors on its summit, believed in the eighteenth century to be Druids' altars, where human sacrifices were made in pre-Christian times. No longer dominating the mountain top, the three rocks are over-shadowed today by complex communications pylons erected by various agencies such as Bord Telecom and the Gardai; one of them serves a radio link for doctors' emergencies in the Dublin area.

A steady climb to the south over a track that is often mucky will bring you to the Fairy Castle, the remains of an ancient burial cairn now surmounted by an Ordnance Survey level mount. From here the views to the south are extensive; from the familiar Sugar Loaf the main nearby peaks East to West are Maulin, behind which rise Djouce and War Hill, Tonduff and Kippure, identified by the TV mast.

Leaving the Fairy Castle, follow the Wicklow Way west and then south down into the valley of Glendoo. On reaching the road the Wicklow Way turns left towards the townland of Ballybrack.

KILMASHOGUE CIRCUIT
from Kilmashogue car park

This round trip, taking no longer than an hour and a half, ascends to the summit of Kilmashogue and returns to the car park via Kelly's Glen. Leaving the car park, take the upper or right hand forestry road and follow it through mixed wood-land and banks of wood sorrel up the side of the mountain. As the track emerges from the forest, it passes through a gateway. Seventy yards on, fork to the right beside another gateway and follow a pathway up the mountain side parallel with a stone wall. It is quite a steep climb, but if the weather is good there are plenty of opportunities to pause for breath and admire the extensive view opening up to the north and east.

Before long, the stone cairn that stands near the summit comes into view ahead. Carry on over the flat summit and down through the heather on the far side. Aim for the dip on the skyline to the right of the Fairy Castle, that prominent cairn on the ridge ahead. The going is a little rough here, so take your time and watch as you go for the hares and grouse that frequent these uplands.

The hare, although similar to a rabbit, is a lot bigger, and while rabbits shelter underground, the hare shapes a nest in the open grass called a form. During the mating season hares can be seen to leap and kick and have boxing matches with each other — a spectacular sight.

Red grouse are not easily seen on the ground because of their effective camouflage; the first sign you usually get of their presence is an explosive flapping as they take to the air and speed away with fast wingbeats, often with a mocking laughlike call. Heather is the mainstay of the grouse's existence; they use it for cover, they nest in it and it is their main staple food all year round.

When you meet the newly made track crossing the south slope of the mountain, turn right and it will bring you shortly to the public road, where another right turn will lead you downhill again. The glen to your left is Kelly's Glen where two hundred years ago a spa attracted people from far and wide to take the waters. You could even have a daily delivery of the spa water to your doorstep in Dublin!

On the way down, look out for the old-fashioned weather vane on the gable of the old farmhouse on the left and further on, on the right, a typical US mailbox on the gateway of a modern bungalow.

Soon the Scots pines, larches and holly trees of Larch Hill demesne come into view. This extensive estate is now a Scout and Guide centre, and in holiday time scattered with tents, awnings and elaborate rustic timber camping structures. Less than a half a mile beyond Larch Hill the road reaches Kilmashogue car park.

KELLYSTOWN ROAD CIRCUIT
This circuit departs from the Way in Kilmashogue Wood to return to Marley by way of Three Rock Mountain.

The mountain hare and red grouse in flight

16

Continue following the forest road when the Wicklow Way turns off sharply to the right and at the next fork keep right. Soon the target positions of the old Ticknock military rifle range are passed on the left, before the road up to Three Rock summit is reached; a five minute detour to the right will bring you up to the space-age array of radomes and gantrys there.

Turning left, follow the road downhill and when it reaches a T-junction, cross over and descend the track through the trees, meeting a rough road in about two minutes. Turn left and left again into the trees, thus reaching a tarmacadam road and turn right onto it. In minutes the public road is met; turn right and downhill as the Hill of Howth comes in view across the bay. The extensive brown building with the white roofs in the foreground of the view is the National Mint.

Turn left onto Kellystown Road, a narrow lane bounded on both sides by fence posts made from old bedframes. Many's the bed had to collapse before the livestock around here were secure from wandering! Note the two fairy bushes in the field on the right, before the road descends towards Kellystown. I wonder were the two old bohans on the left, which now serve as the entrance buildings to the Glenross Pitch and Putt Course, the homesteads of the original Kellys? The place is now a pleasant gathering of old and new houses, the older buildings clothed in elderflower and fuchsia.

Beyond Kellystown, Stackstown Golf Club is passed on the left; thirty minutes after leaving the woods, College Road is met near the Marley Park Hotel. Turning left see if you can spot the granite uprights of a portal dolmen called the Brehon's Chair in the grounds to your left; in the last century this was thought to have been the Seat of Judgment of the Arch Druid. A recent planning application for housing in the area plus the threat that the Southern Cross motorway would obliterate the remains led to an archeological dig being carried out around the dolmen. The dig uncovered arrow heads, axeheads and pottery — all evidence that there was a considerable settlement in the area during the Stone Age.

The gates of St Columba's College are passed before the Wicklow Way is rejoined at the back entrance to Marley Park, ten minutes after reaching College Road.

The Brehon's Chair

18

The red stag

GLENDOO VALLEY
to
CURTLESTOWN WOOD ENTRANCE

Glendoo Valley is a beautiful place, where rhododendrons bloom profusely in early summer and ravens, which nest in the high trees, fill the valley with their honking call. On reaching Ballybrack the Wicklow Way turns right and crosses the valley before climbing steeply through the old world atmosphere of Boranaraltry.

In the woods above Boranaraltry you may catch a glimpse of Sika or red deer moving through the trees or across an open space. The red deer is our largest native wild animal and has roamed these mountains for thousands of years. Although called red, they are grey-brown in Winter, with a large white patch around the tail called the 'target'. Their colour is so close to the surroundings they frequent that the movement of this white patch is often the only give-away allowing you to spot them.

Deer have favourite feeding spots and mating areas, and use the same paths over and over. The surface of the forest road here is fine grained and if a little damp, ideal for spotting animal tracks, so even if you don't actually see the inhabitants of the woods, careful observation will tell you what animals have passed by. For other signs of the presence of deer, check for damage to trees along the roadway. Some trees may have been used as rubbing posts, with the bark worn smooth and sometimes a deer's fur caught in the bark. Young trees may have bark stripped by feeding deer, causing them to develop crookedly almost like dwarf trees.

Sika deer are very like red deer, but have spotted coats. One problem that makes identification difficult is the fact that red and Sika deer have been interbred in Wicklow, and there are many hybrids in the area.

A full grown red deer stands about 3' 8" at the shoulder and can weigh up to 250 lb. While this is large in terms of Ireland's

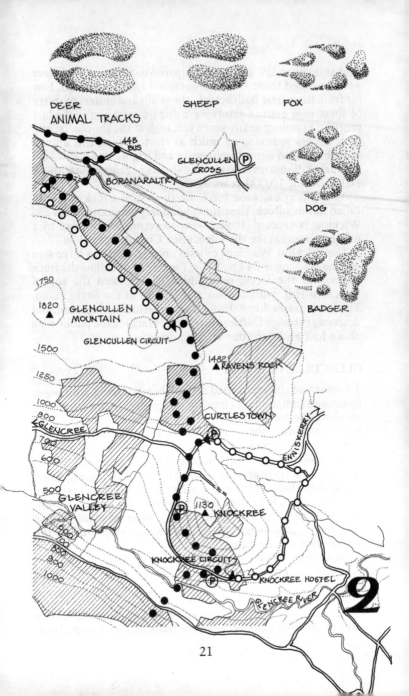

DEER   SHEEP   FOX

ANIMAL TRACKS

44B
BUS

GLENCULLEN
CROSS ℗

BORANARALTRY

DOG

1820 ▲ GLENCULLEN
MOUNTAIN

GLENCULLEN CIRCUIT

BADGER

1482 ▲ RAVENS ROCK

1500

1250

CURTLESTOWN

ENNISKERRY →

GLENCREE →

700
600

500

GLENCREE
VALLEY

℗ 1130 ▲ KNOCKREE

KNOCKREE CIRCUIT

℗

△ KNOCKREE HOSTEL

GLENCREE RIVER

2

wild animals today, it is tiny compared to the great Irish deer which roamed these same mountains 11,000 years ago. Not far from here, near Ballybetagh, the skulls and antlers of thirty of these now extinct giants were dug out of a bog in the last century. Standing nearly seven feet high at the shoulders, and with antlers spanning as much as thirteen feet, this animal must have been a most impressive and frightening sight. Like the earlier dinosaurs, the great Irish deer became mysteriously extinct about 10,000 years ago.

As the Way exits the forest north west of a rocky outcrop called Raven's Rock, the county boundary between Dublin and Wicklow is crossed. If you want to return to the road by a different route, take the Glencullen Circuit (see below).

The Wicklow Way now crosses open ground to a large sign which says Moyne 74 km. Cross the fence and follow the track down into the trees, over which can be seen the top of Knockree Hill, with Maulin and Djouce in the background. The track passes down through a fine natural rock garden, and descends through Curtlestown Wood reaching the public road about half an hour after starting down.

GLENCULLEN CIRCUIT

To return to the main road at Ballybrack, taking a different route, and completing a circuit in under three hours, turn right up along the forest edge and right again at the corner of the forest, following the track between the fence and the trees towards the northwest.

The ground here is very mucky in places and if it becomes too much so, there are a number of forest roads leading down to the right that will bring you back to the Wicklow Way. The wet black peat of the track here, however, contains many well-defined animal tracks, particularly those of deer, whose presence is also suggested by the damage displayed by the young trees on the right.

Prominent signs indicate that the lands to the south are private and a game reserve. The number of deer passing here regularly and the plentiful grouse in the area must make this reserve a game shooting paradise.

The track becomes a deep pond at one stage and you have to take to the drier bank between the track and the forest. At the

22

pond the mountains of Glendoo and Tibradden come into view ahead.

The cairn on Tibradden is said to have been raised over the grave of Nial Glendubh, a prominent chieftain who was slain in a battle with the Danes of Dublin at Kilmashogue in the tenth century.

About thirty minutes after leaving the Way a forest roadway is crossed and the track now dips down into a deep picturesque ravine to cross a stream by stepping stones. After a further ten minutes you enter the forest again and following the forestry road around in a loop to the right, the Wicklow Way is rejoined above Boranaraltry.

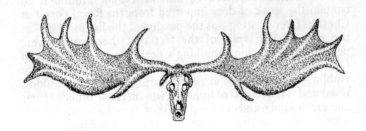

Antlers of the great Irish deer

CURTLESTOWN WOOD
to
CRONE WOOD

Leaving Curtlestown Wood, turn right onto the road and take the next left turn leading across Glencree Valley by way of Knockree.

Although sparsely forested now, the valley of Glencree was clothed 700 years ago by thick woodland stretching westwards as far as the slopes of Lough Bray below Kippure. The very holly trees along the roadside here at Knockree are probably the descendants of those which grew in the valley when Glencree was declared a Royal Park in the thirteenth century and an extensive fenced embankment built around it to contain the stock of deer imported from the Royal Forest at Chester. Deer hunting was the passion of the English kings at the time, and in spite of the fact that there were severe penalties for poaching the king's deer, the royal animals in Glencree were never safe! Even the Abbot of St Mary's in Dublin, who had lands at neighbouring Glencullen couldn't resist and was accused of hunting 'with nets and other engines and greyhounds, and of taking wild beasts and working his will with them to the great injury of our Lord the King'.

Time was running out however for the Irish forests. The popularity of Irish oak for building (in the twelfth century it was used in the construction of Westminster Hall and of many of the major Norman castles of England and Wales) and the enormous quantities of it that went towards the expansion of the English navy saw Ireland's woodland disappear in decades. The last of the extensive woods were destroyed in Elizabethan times to deny shelter to the rebellious Irish, and to feed the increasing number of ironworks with the charcoal they required.

All that remains today of the Royal Park of Glencree are the great tree stumps found from time to time in the bog near Lough Bray, a surviving section of embankment near Curtlestown, and a few holly and oak trees, descendants of the original trees, scattered around the valley competing with the modern forestry.

Wooden bridge over the Glencree River

25

Halfway across the valley, the Wicklow Way turns left into the forest for a while, before crossing the road again to descend to the Glencree River. At the road, a return can be made to Curtlestown Wood by another route; see Knockree Circuit below. This area has a rich mixture of both deciduous and coniferous trees; children can compete in numbering and identifying the species encountered between the road and the river, amongst which will be seen holly, beech, oak, cypress, Norway, spruce, cedar and Scots pine.

The Way crosses the Glencree River over a picturesque if rickety wooden structure like one of the jungle bridges from the movies.

The route now ascends through woodbine-wreathed trees and very boggy ground to the public road above. There are many tracks going uphill and each time I walk this section I find myself on a different one, following any direction that appears to avoid the worst of the wet ground. If you go a little astray this way, just remember the road is only a few hundred yards uphill and hard to miss. The Wicklow Way continues across the road under a tall lone cypress tree.

After a short steep climb straight up from the public road a forestry road is met. Turn left and head towards Crone Wood through an area of forest which at time of writing is being harvested. After crossing a concrete bridge over a stream, the road forks; take the right fork up into an area of well-spaced Corsican and Scots pines planted some time during the last war. Some trees here carry signs indicating their height and the volume of timber they contain.

After a short downhill stretch that brings you within five minutes of Crone Wood car park, the Way begins to ascend again.

KNOCKREE CIRCUIT

This circuit is almost entirely on the public roadway and makes a pleasant walk of about two hours at any time of the year.

Instead of continuing the Wicklow Way down to the Glencree River, turn left along the road after coming down out of Knockree Wood. Knockree Youth Hostel is passed on the left after a short while. Further on look out for a portal dolmen forming part of the boundary between two fields; land clearance around here, however, has resulted in what could be dolmens everywhere you look. The real dolmen is about 100 feet to the right of the road, near a white-washed cottage with a black roof.

After a while a crag called Raven's Rock appears on the skyline ahead, and the road bears right and down into a hollow between high holly hedges to cross a small stone bridge. Take a left fork at the old schoolhouse at the top of the hill, and after a short distance turn sharp left after a bungalow into an old boreen, a little piece of nineteenth-century Ireland. Gradually the boreen widens until, tarmacadam covered, its northern end becomes the entrance road to some fine new bungalows.

You should reach the main road again about an hour after departing from the Wicklow Way. Turn left and head towards Curtlestown, passing the school and church on the right.

Near the church is the old national school carefully added to and re-furbished as a dwelling house. Curtlestown cemetery, in use since the late nineteenth century rises up the hill behind the church.

The Wicklow Way is rejoined at Curtlestown Wood and followed back across Knockree to your starting point.

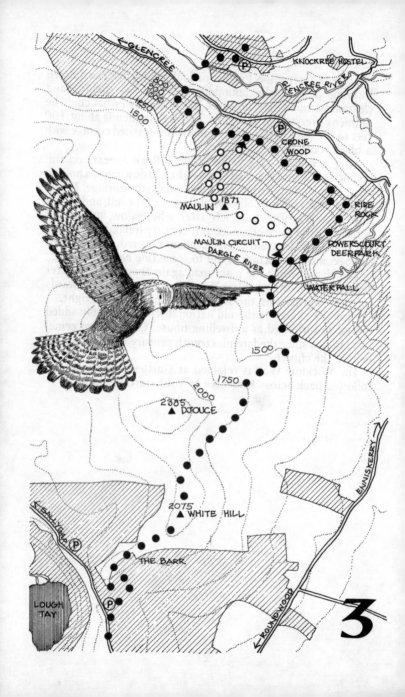

GLENCREE

KNOCKREE HOSTEL

GLENCREE RIVER

1250

1500

(P)

CRONE WOOD

MAULIN ▲ 1871

RIDE ROCK

MAULIN CIRCUIT
DARGLE RIVER

POWERSCOURT DEERPARK

WATERFALL

1500

1750

2000

▲ 2385 DJOUCE

▲ 2075 WHITE HILL

THE BARR

(P)

LOUGH TAY

ENNISKERRY

ROUNDWOOD

3

CRONE WOOD
to
LUGGALA GATES

The Wicklow Way climbs evenly through Crone Wood for a further 30 minutes and shortly after glimpsing Great Sugar Loaf to the left framed by conifers, the route arrives quite suddenly out of the forest at Ride Rock, a cliff top promontory with a breathtaking panorama of Powerscourt Deerpark. The view sweeps around from Carrickgollogan past the majestic Sugar Loaf to the great waterfall crashing noisily over the cliff into the Glen below, with Djouce Mountain behind.

Powerscourt waterfall has been a tourist attraction since first mentioned in the earliest Wicklow Guides in the nineteenth century. Here the River Dargle plunges over 800 feet into the Glen and then meanders its way past the remains of Lord Powerscourt's banqueting hall towards the sea at Bray.

Powerscourt gets its name from a Le Paor who came into possession of the lands here on marrying a daughter of one of Strongbow's followers. A castle was built to help keep in check the Wicklow clans of the O'Tooles and O'Byrnes who for centuries sent marauding expeditions against the foreigners occupying Dublin from the safety of their bases in the Wicklow wilderness. Tirlagh O'Toole himself was granted the castle and lands one time in a Machiavellian move, on condition that he and his family would adopt English language and customs, and behave themselves generally. Somehow, the O'Tooles managed to fulfil at least the spirit of this agreement for sixty years, before they fell from favour again and retreated into the mountains.

For his prowess on behalf of the Crown in fighting the French and putting down Irish rebellions, Sir Richard Wingfield was granted the lands in the early seventeenth century and was later created Lord Powerscourt. His descendants developed the lands, laid out the elaborate gardens and built the magnificent Powerscourt House, which was renowned for its fine interiors and its original furnishings until it was unfortunately destroyed by fire some years ago.

When King George IV visited Ireland in 1821, he was entertained at Powerscourt to a banquet. A special viewing bridge was erected in the Glen for him to see the waterfall, but he had to leave without doing so. To really impress him, the Dargle had been dammed above the waterfall to be released spectacularly for the King. Just as well he missed it, for when the torrent was released, it thundered dramatically over the cliff and carried the viewing bridge completely away!

The pathway the Wicklow Way follows around the Glen provides an unusual viewpoint for bird-watching, a real 'bird's-eye' view, looking down on the tree tops. Wood pigeons and crows can be seen below moving about from tree to tree, and the occasional hen harrier cruises back and forth searching out prey.

Red deer and Sika deer often browse on the steep treed sides of the glen below the path. When disturbed they will go bounding downwards to cover, their white tail patches the only clearly identifiable shape against the background.

Before reaching the waterfall, the Wicklow Way turns right into the forest. At time of writing thinning of the trees has all but obliterated the track, but if in doubt, head the easiest way you can find down towards the western edge of the wood which is only a couple of hundred yards away, running parallel to the now dilapidated Powerscourt Demesne Wall. Emerging from the trees at the wall the vast desolate Dargle valley opens up ahead, with Djouce Mountain and War Hill on its south side and Maulin and Tonduff on the north.

Before the Famine this valley had a small population of cottiers and in winter when the bracken is low the shape of the remains of their dwellings can be spotted, together with the evidence of their labour, parallel 'lazy beds' or wide potato drills extending considerable distances up the mountain slopes. To return to Crone Wood car park from here via Maulin will take under two hours, see Maulin Circuit (page 32).

Turn left and make your way downhill along the old stone wall towards the Dargle River, which gives no hint here that within a few hundred yards it will abruptly plummet over the cliff into Powerscourt Glen. At time of writing the timber bridge that crossed the Dargle here, swept away during Hurricane Charlie, has not been replaced, but except after heavy rainfall it should be possible to cross the stepping stones without getting your feet wet. Follow the boggy track uphill now beside the old wall and around to the left at the corner of the wood. Within a few minutes the Way turns right and heads south across the heather towards Djouce Mountain. In spring and summer this place is filled with lark song, as everywhere skylarks rise up vertically into the air proclaiming their territory.

Within about forty-five minutes of crossing the Dargle you should pass a well-beaten track leading uphill to the right, towards the summit of Djouce (2,385 ft) about a third of a mile to the north west. The views down to the coast from here on the mountain side are extensive; the Kish lighthouse appears to be surprisingly close inshore, while any shipping movements within thirty miles of the coast can be clearly monitored on a good day — indeed if weather conditions are reasonable, Wales should be visible on the eastern horizon.

Passing by the turnoff for the summit of Djouce, the Wicklow Way ascends to 2,075 ft at White Hill, probably named for the gleaming outcrops of quartz and schist scattered over the mountainside here. Watch out for the hazardous remains of old iron fence posts protruding from the ground on or near the track. To the north west Kippure with its TV mast comes into view, while to the south east Wicklow Head is easily identified on the coast.

Descending from White Hill along the Barr, another of the Wicklow Way's sudden and spectacular vistas opens up. The view to the south takes in layer after layer of mountain range, while in the middle distance Lough Dan darkly glints, and 600 feet below at the foot of the cliffs of Fancy is Lough Tay, with its fine beach on the northern side. A few minutes' stop to identify the visible peaks is worthwhile here before descending to the public road. In the foreground is Fancy or Luggala (1,956 ft) and to its left with a rugged top is Knocknacloghoge. Further left, reaching to the skyline is Scarr (2,108 ft). In clear weather the most recognisable of the further-off mountains is Turlough Hill, with the reservoir on its summit seen as a long, perfectly flat plateau with a little tower. To the left of Turlough Hill is Tonelagee (2,686 ft) and to its right beyond, the unimpressive looking bump that is Wicklow's highest mountain, Lugnaquillia (3,039 ft).

The valley between Lough Tay and Lough Dan has some of the finest scenery in the county. Concealed under the shoulder of the north eastern side of the valley is Luggala Lodge, built by the La Touches of Marlay as a hunting lodge, and there can be few country houses in Ireland in such an idyllic setting.

While descending the mountainside here, watch out for one of Ireland's rarest birds, the peregrine falcon, which has been known to nest on the crags over Lough Tay. The peregrine is quite a large bird whose wingspan can be in excess of 3′ 6″ and it preys on other birds such as wood pigeon and wild duck. It kills its victim dramatically on the wing after a dive or 'stoop' from above in which it can attain speeds of up to 100 miles per hour. Although the peregrine sometimes soars, it is usually seen to fly with swift wingbeats interrupted occasionally by short glides.

The Wicklow Way descends to the public road and on down to the stone piered gates of the Luggala Estate, opposite which there is parking for a few cars.

MAULIN CIRCUIT

On exiting the forest, turn right up the hill along the old Powerscourt Demesne wall, and on reaching the highest point of the ridge look for a track going left up towards Maulin summit and follow it; the top is less than thirty minutes away. Watch out for red grouse and hares, usually plentiful in the area. The views from this ridge are dramatic; the treeless mountain wilderness to the south contrasts sharply with the forested and cultivated valley and hills to the north.

To the north east the grey-walled remains of Powerscourt House can be seen with Carrickgollogan beyond. The sea coast of Wicklow can now be seen extending to Wicklow Head and beyond.

The summit of Maulin at 1,817 feet above sea level is marked by a cairn of glittering mica schist.

To return to Crone car park, head downhill towards the north east through an opening in the low stone wall just below the summit, and then go down steeply through thick heather towards the nearest forest edge. Move slowly and carefully, as there are occasional holes and rocks to catch the unsuspecting foot. This is one place you will find a walking stick comes in

Peregrine falcon

33

very useful. Within about fifteen minutes a forest track at the edge of the trees is reached. Turn left and then right, and keep zigzagging down the hillside; at junctions always take the descending route no matter what direction it takes. Within about forty-five minutes of leaving the summit you should re-connect with the Wicklow Way route. Crone Wood car park is now about fifteen minutes away to the east.

The hen harrier

LUGGALA GATES
to
OLDBRIDGE CROSS

The Wicklow Way continues past a further gateway, inscribed Ballinrush Cottage, before bearing left and downhill. After a minute or two, the route leaves the public road and enters Sleamaine Wood on the right. Originally the Wicklow Way followed the public road all the way to Oldbridge and then on to Paddock Hill, making six miles in all on tarmac. This welcome revision takes you up onto the flanks of Ballinafunshogue Hill before returning to the road at Ashtown.

Follow the wide forestry road, passing through two timber gateways while the Vartry Reservoir at Roundwood comes into view to the south east. Fed by the Vartry River which rises at the base of Great Sugar Loaf Mountain (now coming into view behind) the reservoir can contain over 6,000 million gallons of water. On a clear day the Irish Sea and the Wicklow coast is visible from here for many miles to the south; the outskirts of Wicklow town can be easily identified perched on the north slopes of Ballyguile Hill.

Passing through sections of mature and recently planted forestry, turn right at the next T-junction and ascend towards the west. The forestry road has been cut into the hillside here and it is possible to see that the peat in which the trees spread their roots is not much more than twelve inches deep in places.

Topping a rise onto the open hillside the rugged ridge of Scarr Mountain comes into view, with Tonelagee in the background. On the left the patchwork pattern of fertile fields and woodland stretching eastwards from Roundwood is a total contrast to the desolate ruggedness of the mountain scenery on the right.

The forest road loops around under ESB wires serving the valley below and less than ten minutes later the route passes through a cleared area with minor forest tracks to the left and right. For the Lough Dan alternative (page 39) which describes an alternative route to Oldbridge, and the Cloghoge Circuit (page 38) which drops down into the valley before

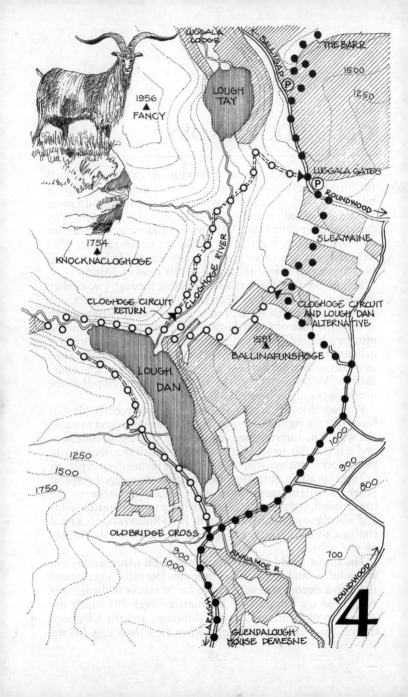

FANCY ▲ 1956

LUGGALA LODGE

R. SLUGGAP

THE BARR
1500
1250

LOUGH TAY

KNOCKNACLOGHOGE ▲ 1754

LUGGALA GATES

P ROUNDWOOD →

SLEAMAINE

CLOGHOGE CIRCUIT RETURN

R. CLOGHOGE RIVER

CLOGHOGE CIRCUIT AND LOUGH DAN ALTERNATIVE

BALLINAFUNSHOGE ▲ 1581

LOUGH DAN

1000

1250
1500
1750

900
800

OLDBRIDGE CROSS

ANNAMOE R.

ROUNDWOOD

700

900
1000

↓ LARAGH

GLENDALOUGH HOUSE DEMESNE

4

returning up to the public road at the gates of the Luggala Estate, leave the Wicklow Way route by taking the sharp right turn here.

Although it is said that coniferous woods discourage birdlife, the theory is not borne out here in summertime, when the air is full of birdsong — robins, wrens, great tits, chaffinches, blackbirds and thrushes all insisting on a hearing. While most people will recognise the robin's song, it takes much time and patience to learn to identify each species' song. While identifying which song comes from which bird can be difficult, children can have fun making up phrases that suit the rhythm and tone of particular bird calls. For instance the chaffinch call sounds like 'What-what-what-what d'you r-r-r-really think of ME now' while the song thrush's offering sounds like 'Did-he-do-it, he did, he did, he did.'

The forestry road soon emerges on to the open hillside again with good views down to Vartry Reservoir to the left. I understand it is eventually hoped to keep straight on here, over Ballinafunshogue and down to a point where Lough Dan is overlooked, before returning to the public road just before Oldbridge. For the present however, a post directs you to the left off the forestry road over a gate into a field. Carry on downhill beside the forest edge. About halfway down the field turn south and follow a rough track that soon becomes a boreen. Cross a gate in the boreen and continue past the ruins of a stone cottage; look out for the remains of a finely made old iron mangle in the hedge on the left. In the old days these machines were used to shred root crops to provide feed for pigs and young livestock. A cluster of picturesque red-roofed whitewashed cottages are passed on the left before the boreen drops down to a T-junction where the Wicklow Way turns right.

Although a bleak spot in winter, this road is quite lush in summertime, with abundant hawthorn, blackthorn, holly, willow, mountain ash and hazel trees, many garlanded with strings of fragant woodbine. There is a theory that hedgerows gain one new species of shrub or tree every hundred years, allowing a roadway to be dated. This road is supposed to be very old, so a good place to test the theory; count the number of different varieties in a 40-pace stretch — the number will suggest the age of the hedgerow in hundreds of years. The test

37

should be done at a number of places along the road.

One of the bungalows on the right here has a small museum of gaily painted antique agricultural machinery laid out on its lawns. Keep straight until the road forks at a house called 'Village View', take the right fork and at the next junction take the turn signposted 'Lough Dan'.

The road descends into an oak wood, thickly planted with moss and lichen covered trees, under which lies a carpet of fraughans from which the harvest must be considerable in August. Small herds of deer often browse here, well camouflaged in the dappled sunlight.

A little further on there is a bridge over the Avonmore River, which, after joining the Avoca River, reaches the sea at Arklow. It is said there was a bridge in this place since ancient times when the road here was the main road connecting Glendalough with the monasteries at Tallaght and Clondalkin. A few minutes later Oldbridge Cross is reached where the Lough Dan Alternative rejoins the Way, opposite the entrance gates and quaint gatehouse to Glendalough House.

CLOGHOGE CIRCUIT

This is a three hour circuit descending into the Cloghoge River Valley amidst some of the finest scenery in the Wicklow Mountains and returning back up to the public road.

Leaving the Wicklow Way north of Ballinafunshogue follow the route described in the Lough Dan Alternative (page 39) until the River Cloghoge is crossed near its entry to Lough Dan. Now turning right follow the stone-walled roadway northwards. After about ten minutes you pass the place where a land slip swept away the road when Hurricane Charlie struck in 1986, exposing thousands of tons of unweathered clean granite, schist and quartz.

Watch out for small herds of deer along here, either well camouflaged in the bracken above the road, or grazing like sheep in the meadow below. A few shaggy long-haired wild goats inhabit the cliffs along the east of the valley and pheasants, which are bred here, can sometimes be seen in large numbers.

The pheasant originated in the Far East and first appeared in the British Isles in the eleventh century. The cock is a most colourful bird with exotic plumage, a blue-green head and long trailing tail feathers, while the hen is a much plainer flecked grey-brown colour, which helps her to become almost invisible when nesting on the ground. While pheasants are extremely shy and wary during the shooting season, they seem to know when it is over and can become quite daring and unconcerned by man's proximity.

Keep to the roadway, crossing wooden bridges — first over a tributary and then over the Cloghoge River. Ascend the hill past the farm buildings and a white-washed cottage down to your left, which make a most picturesque scene in springtime as the entire area in front of the cottage is devoted to a daffodil 'crop'.

The Wicklow Way is rejoined at the public road at the top of the hill.

LOUGH DAN ALTERNATIVE
from Luggala Gates to Oldbridge

This is an alternative route to Oldbridge making a circuit of Wicklow's largest lake and taking about four hours. The route involves crossing the Cloghoge River by stepping stones, so after periods of heavy rainfall or melting of snow be prepared to retrace your steps if the river is in flood. After turning sharp right off the Wicklow Way, within five minutes you meet the fence at the edge of the forest. Turn left and follow the fence uphill, crossing another fence across the path and exiting onto a heather-covered hillside newly planted with spruce trees, with Ballinafunshoge rising up in the background. Crossing a wooden gate at a point where Lough Dan, with the beach at its western end, comes into view, take the almost overgrown middle one of the three possible tracks across the heather-covered hillside. The great bulk of Knocknacloghoge with its rugged quartz top now looms to the right; look for a grey strain on its flanks where a massive landslip occurred during the height of Hurricane Charlie in 1986.

As the hillside is crossed the rugged beauty of this valley begins to unfold with Lough Tay coming into view to the north, the cliffs of Fancy towering over it. When the track reaches the forest edge, turn right and follow it downhill. On the way down on your right look out for a boulder perched precariously on top of another. This phenomenon, a product of the Ice Ace, occurs frequently in this area; the melting ice sheet deposited one boulder on the other, sometimes so delicately that the upper one can be rotated with a slight push. A massive 'rotating stone' said to have been used by the Druids for ceremonies, existed not far from here, until upset by a passing company of soldiers early in the last century.

At the bottom of the steep incline you come to a stone-walled grassed boreen. Turn left and follow the boreen down past the ruins of a pre-famine cottage and through a small mature wood of larches and Scots pines. Look out for squirrels here; the ground is littered with stripped larch cones and red squirrels can often be sighted. When the 'green' boreen joins a gravel road, turn left. The rapids of the Cloghoge River should be audible now as you turn right before the gates of Ballinrush Cottage and descend along the boundary; look out for an old timber-built threshing machine in the farmyard on your left. The track comes out of the trees onto the banks of the Cloghoge River, opposite a white-washed hostel building. It is often possible to cross the river on the stones where the 'rapids' begin, but to be sure to keep your footwear dry, it is wiser to tackle the crossing barefoot; be brave, it can be very cold.

This is an ideal place in good weather to sit awhile and take in the surroundings. Yellow wagtails and dippers are common on the river here, while ravens can often be seen soaring over the hillside above. Chaffinches, long-tailed tits and coat tits are common in the willow groves along the river.

Head west along the lake shore through the gorse bushes. Soon you will pass the end of the lake with its idyllic white beach. Continue westwards along the Inchavore River; to avoid the extensive boggy ground, either keep on the river bank as it meanders along, or ascend to the rock scree and move from rock to tock.

You will soon reach another old ruined cottage near the river. This one was constructed in such harmony with its site that it's hard to know where the bedrock ends and the man-made masonry begins.

Old threshing machine near the Cloghoge River

Below the cottage, cross the river by stepping stones onto a stony beach made up of gleaming rounded granite 'eggs' delved up by Hurricane Charlie.

Before turning east and setting off down the southern side of Lough Dan, a small detour is worthwhile; head for the grove of deciduous trees a few hundred yards to the west. Here, in a copse of oak, willow and larch trees, the river Inchavore tumbles through the rocks, forming numerous tiny bathing places for summertime use. A large granite boulder bears a carved welcome message; this is an ideal place for a picnic.

Leaving this grove, head eastwards towards the boreen winding up the hillside ahead. In one of the deserted cottages at the beginning of the boreen survives a rare mud and wattle chimney gathering, suspended over the fireplace to collect the smoke and channel it out through the roof.

Follow the boreen up the hillside past a grove of spruce trees and a beautifully sited cottage. The views over the lake here are magnificent and provide plenty of excuses to stop for a breath; keep a lookout for rabbits in the fields to the left. After topping the hill, the boreen bears around to the right and passing a farmhouse, drops down to a stile onto a public road. Turning left follow the public road back to Oldbridge, now just a mile away.

OLDBRIDGE CROSS
to
LARAGH

Leaving the Cross ascend the steep hill beside Glendalough House Demesne wall. Erskine Childers, father of the late President and famed for his gun-running exploits on the yacht Asgard in 1914, was a frequent visitor to Glendalough House, the home of his cousin Robert Barton. It was here that he was arrested by government troops during the Civil War, and found to have in his possession a small revolver given to him by Michael Collins a year before. Carrying arms was a capital offence, and in spite of many pleas for leniency, this brave Englishman was executed a few days later, after shaking hands with each member of the firing squad.

The road descends again and crosses a stream. About a hundred yards from the stream, opposite a bright red wooden gate a side road leads west. If you would like an alternative to the next mile and a half on the public road, taking you up onto the ridge above and rejoining the Wicklow Way at Paddock Hill, see Paddock Hill Alternative (on page 45).

As the trees of Glendalough House Demesne are left behind and the road runs out into open country, three hills can be seen to the south and east. The middle one, Castle Kevin, was as far as Red Hugh O'Donnell got after his first spectacular escape from Dublin Castle in the winter of 1590. He had been heading for the sanctuary of Fiach McHugh O'Byrne's territory in Glenmalure when, suffering from exhaustion, he was forced to ask the local chief, Phelim O'Toole, for assistance. But O'Toole was a weak-willed man and, anxious to offend neither his English neighbours to the north, nor his fellow Wicklowmen to the south, he sent out two messengers with the news of Red Hugh, a slow one to the English and a fast one to Glenmalure. The rivers however were in flood and held up the fast messenger and when O'Byrne's men arrived at Castle Kevin, they found the English had already taken Red Hugh back to Dublin. Almost exactly a year later, the young prince again escaped from his captors, this time avoiding O'Toole

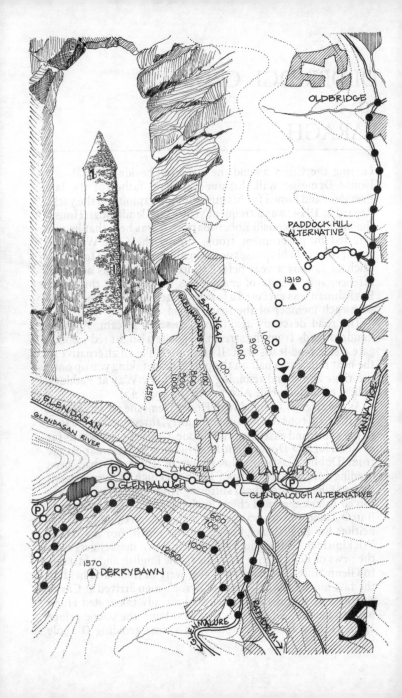

OLDBRIDGE

PADDOCK HILL
ALTERNATIVE

1319

GLENDASAN R.

SALLYGAP

1000

900

800

700

600

500

1000

1250

GLENDASAN

GLENDASAN RIVER

P   P   HOSTEL

GLENDALOUGH

ANNAMOE

LARAGH   P

GLENDALOUGH ALTERNATIVE

P   P

500

700

1000

1250

1570

DERRYBAWN

KINGMALURE

AVONMORE R.

5

territory and successfully reaching Glenmalure.

Having passed a stone-walled boreen leading left down to Annamoe, the rolling pasture and treed slopes of Paddock Hill can be seen ahead. Where the forest comes down to the road the Wicklow Way turns right and heads up through the trees to exit onto the green hillside just south of the summit. Laragh can be seen below in the valley, with the wooded steep slopes of Derrybawn Mountain in the background.

A short distance downhill the Wicklow Way veers to the right and crosses the heather into the trees. Descending steeply through the wood and crossing a stile onto the public road, turn left and within minutes turn right off the road again, crossing a stile into the woods. The Way now crosses a picturesque wooden bridge over the Glenmacnass River, and within a few minutes becomes a forestry track, before reaching the western edge of the wood, where a sign indicates that Marley is now 51.75 km away. Turning left, the Way follows an old Mass path down to the village of Laragh.

Due to its important position on the crossing of the Glenmacnass River, Laragh was one of the locations where Military Barracks were erected after the 1798 Rebellion, to control the county and protect the new military road that had been built deep into the heart of Wicklow. Within fifty years a thriving village had grown up with a mill, a church and of course a public house. Today Laragh is a pleasant spacious village, taking full advantage of the proximity of Glendalough and the mountains, providing refreshments and accommodation for an increasing number of tourists every year.

PADDOCK HILL ALTERNATIVE

This route avoids the next mile and a half on the public road and takes you up on the ridge to rejoin the Way at Paddock Hill.

Turn up the unsurfaced road heading south. After about fifteen minutes you reach a gate, beyond which the track takes three directions. Follow the left-hand one, cross a stile and ascend the track parallel to the fence. On reaching the brow of the hill, turn right off the track and head towards the highest point, taking care with your footing, as the ground can be rough.

In summertime this hillside is absolutely alive with larks, which rise up ahead of you, singing indignantly at your audacity in approaching their nests. Sometimes they will make a very elaborate display to attract your attention and land on a tuft of heather near you, hoping to lead you away from the nest.

Another bird that can often be seen here is the kestrel, Ireland's commonest falcon; it is easily identified by its habit of hovering almost motionless twenty or thirty feet from the ground as it searches for prey. The hovering kestrel is always a perfect wind-vane as it always faces into the wind, using its broad tail for stability. This bird of prey feeds mainly on mice and large insects, whose movements on the ground are spotted while the bird hovers noiselessly above. Kestrels suffered a sharp decline during the sixties due to argicultural use of chemicals like DDT, but they are now on the increase again, and can even be seen in cities.

From the summit the wood on Paddock Hill can be seen to the south, but if you head westwards roughly in line with the two large boulders that can be seen here and cross a fence you will meet a track within a couple of hundred yards. Turn left along this track and head towards Paddock Hill. Below on the right is the valley of Glenmacnass with a geometric patchwork pattern of trees clothing the sides.

You should reach the forest edge where a stile crosses the fence; at this stile you rejoin the Wicklow Way, a little over an hour after leaving it.

LARAGH
to
DRUMGOFF

Heading south out of Laragh on the Rathdrum road, the Glendesan river is crossed again at Bookeys Bridge, after which the unusual Italian style design of Derrybawn House can be seen on the right. The original house here was one of the many in the area to be burned during the rebellion of 1798.

Turn off the Rathdrum road and follow the signpost for Glenmalure at the next junction, entering Derrybawn Wood. Before long, the Wicklow Way turns right off the road and heads up in a northerly direction through the trees. Glimpses of the Round Tower and the monastic ruins of Glendalough can be seen 400 feet below through the trees, after about a mile.

St Kevin is said to have come to this remote valley in the sixth century to escape the amorous intentions of a woman called Kathleen who made his priestly vows difficult to remember; on one occasion he had to throw himself into a bed of nettles to avoid being seduced! But as Tom Moore's poem recounts, she caught up with him:

> By that lake whose gloomy shore
>   Skylarks never warble o'er
> Where the cliff hangs high and steep
>   Young St Kevin stole to sleep
> 'Here at last' he calmly said
>   'Woman ne'er shall find my bed'
> Ah! the good saint little knew
>   What the wily sex can do.

Finally Kevin is said to have thrown Kathleen in the lake, which cooled her down sufficiently for her to join a convent of nuns.

After some years of peace, Kevin was discovered by a shepherd, and soon an increasing number of people came to get a blessing from the holy man. Before long they built him an oratory which, by the time he died in 617, had become a major monastic settlement.

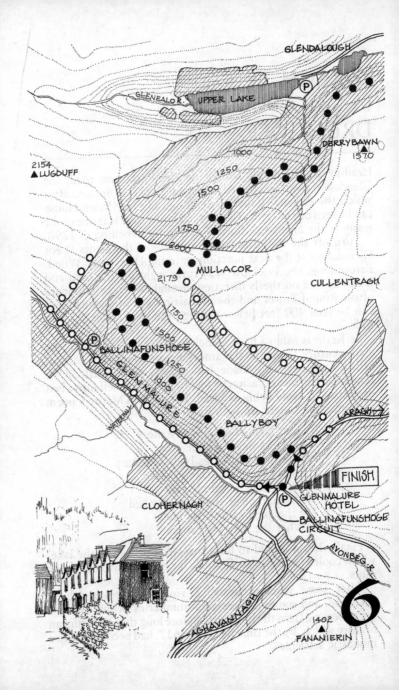

The Wicklow Way continues to circle Derrybawn Mountain, for the most part enclosed by trees, until it exits onto the mountainside to cross the Londuff Brook. The water of the brook has worn down the rocks over which it flows to a smooth undulating staircase, stepping down the hillside in a series of little cascades and pools.

Beyond the bridge over Lugduff Brook, you can see Brockagh Mountain to the north, sloping down towards Laragh nestling at its foot. In the background, the ragged ridge of Scarr Mountain is easily identified. I have found the original Ordnance Survey Wicklow Way map to be inaccurate in showing the route between here and the slopes of Mullacor, so take particular care in following the signposts. Taking a right turn at the next junction and crossing another stream, ascend into a forest of tall mature trees, bearing sharp left at the next fork. In a short time, the Wicklow Way exits the forest into an extensive area that has been recently harvested, leaving a vast silent devastated mountain side. Here more than perhaps any other part of the Wicklow Way there is a tangible sense of remoteness.

After crossing the Lugduff Brook once more the Wicklow Way turns sharply left and then right at the next fork. Thirty yards after the junction, the Wicklow Way leaves the road to follow a steep track up to the left. There are now plenty of opportunities to pause and take in the view, even if only to gather your breath! Camaderry's bulk fills the foreground looking back downhill, while to its left the ESB reservoir, giving Turlough Hill a perfectly flat top, is easily identified.

This short steep stretch shortly reaches another forest road; turn right and after another 100 yards, leave the road again, ascending steeply to the left, up a break in the forest. Turn right at the top and follow the fence up the bare eastern slopes of Mullacor. Magnificent views now open up to the north east; Kippure with its mast can be seen almost thirteen miles away, and if you follow the line of Lugduff eastwards the Lower Lake at Glendalough can be seen at its foot.

The fence eventually turns around to the left and disappears downhill in an easterly direction; however a couple of bare fence posts point the way west to the summit, which is now about 400 yards away.

The summit of Mullacor is unmarked, just a flat boggy

plateau, but as soon as you can see the horizon through 360° you can assume you're there. And what a horizon! Numerous mountain peaks, layer on layer, stretch into the distance south, west and north. In particular look for the rounded heap of Mount Leinster to the south; it is about thirty miles away. Nearer and towards the west is Wicklow's highest peak, Lugnaquillia at 3,039 ft; it is said that you can see five counties from the summit.

A mile or two to the west of Mullacor there is a bog on the mountain side called the Hag's Sloughs, where in ancient times it is said a witch called Cainech came to a horrible end! Legend has it that the King of Leinster gave his son as a foster-ling to St Kevin at Glendalough. The child's mother, Cainech, however was a follower of the 'old religion', and preferred her son to die rather than live as a Christian. On the nearby mountainside, in sight of the seven churches of Glendalough, she began to call upon her gods to strike her child down dead. Down in the monastery, the boy was immediately taken ill, but St Kevin, sensing that a spell was being put on the child, knelt and prayed to counteract it. The saint's magic must have been the strongest, because the mountainside suddenly opened under Cainech and swallowed her up, never to be seen again!

The Wicklow Way continues west down from the summit of Mullacor for about ten minutes, until it reaches a track marked by posts, crossing from north to south. Turn left onto this track and follow the pointers down into the wood, turning left onto the first forestry road you meet. You have now entered the western end of Ballinafunshogue Wood which covers nearly three square miles of the northern side of Glenmalure Valley.

The Wicklow Way now follows a series of forestry roads south east and slowly down across Ballinafunshogue and Ballyboy, giving fine views down into Glenmalure and south-wards towards the south Wicklow peaks.

While ravens can be seen in many places along the Wicklow Way route, I have found that nowhere are you more guaranteed to see them than in Glenmalure. The raven is often not noticed because at a distance he looks very similar to his more common cousins the rook and the hooded crow. His diamond shaped tail, his large black down-curved beak and his great size, sometimes as long as two feet, are the main distinguishing

Ravens in flight

features, but it is usually the bird's resonant hollow 'honking' call that attracts my attention.

Ravens are usually seen singly or in pairs, and if you watch for a while, you will see them perform intricate aerobatics like a snap roll where the bird flips upside down in level flight and a vertical dive performed by tucking his wings in close to his body and plummeting earthwards, only to recover to a soaring climb. To watch a pair of ravens enjoying an intricate choreography of these aerial stunts together is one of the great pleasures of the mountains.

After a few short uphill stretches, the Wicklow Way finally makes its descent down Ballyboy towards the public road, which is reached about an hour and a half after entering the wood. Turn right and descend towards Drumgoff crossroads; fifty yards to the right of the crossroads is the Glenmalure Hotel, an old-world establishment which probably originally started life as a shebeen serving the soldiers of Drumgoff Barracks in the early nineteenth century.

Just across the river from the hotel stands the gaunt ruin of the barracks which, built after the 1798 rebellion and with the military road and the other barracks built at that time, made it difficult for rebel bands to hide in the Wicklow Mountains. The last of the legendary rebel leaders, Michael Dwyer, lived for a time in Glenmalure; in fact within days of Drumgoff Barracks being first completed, Dwyer blew it up with gunpowder!

Dwyer led a charmed life and constantly foiled attempts by the government forces to capture him dead or alive. On one such occasion he was spending the night in a cottage west of Glenmalure when it was surrounded by militia men (directed there presumably by the ubiquitous Irish informer).

Dwyer refused to surrender and the shooting started, shortly after which the thatched roof of the cottage was set alight. Soon the heat was so great inside that butter which had been stored in the cottage melted and flooded the floor. The rebels finally decided to make a run for it and throwing the door open they were dashing out when Dwyer slipped on the melted butter and fell to the ground. The fall saved his life, for in the next second his companions were mown down by a fusillade of musketfire from the militia. While the muskets were being reloaded, Dwyer leapt to his feet and, under cover of the smoke and flames, got clean away.

52

Drumgoff Barracks

53

Michael Dwyer finally gave himself up two years after the 1798 rebellion had been put down and the authorities were so relieved to receive his surrender that they agreed to commute his death sentence and instead transport him to Botany Bay. In spite of that colony being governed at the time by Captain Bligh (of the good ship Bounty fame) Dwyer must have been a model prisoner, for he was eventually made a Constable and died a pillar of the community in 1825.

There are many fine walks and climbs to be had in and around this historic valley; a route which takes in Glenmalure's main features is described in the Ballinafunshogue Circuit (on page 58).

GLENDALOUGH ALTERNATIVE
Laragh to Wicklow Way

This alternative route takes in the monastic ruins of Glendalough and rejoins the Wicklow Way route in Derrybawn Wood. A circuit from Laragh to Glendalough and back via Derrybawn Wood will take about three hours.

Leave the Wicklow Way by turning right at the Jet station in Laragh. After about fifteen minutes the dramatic steep sides of the valley of Glendalough come into view, as the An Oige Hostel is passed on the right. The first of the monastic ruins you will see is that of Trinity Church, to the left of the road. Further on is the new extensive Interpretive Centre, beyond which is the Royal Hotel, which has been catering for tourists for over 150 years.

Turning sharp left after the hotel, the road crosses the Glendasan River and immediately ahead are the remains of the original arched gatehouse to the monastic settlement. It originally had an upper storey, from where the gatekeeper would operate the mechanism to open and close the gates. Just inside the gatehouse on the right you will see a cross carved on a stone slab. It is said that anyone seeking sanctuary in the monastery of Glendalough was safe from outside interference having passed this cross.

The monastic settlement, founded by St Kevin in the sixth century, is said to have been located to the west near the upper lake, and it was long after his death that the 'city' of Glendalough grew up here dominated by the round tower and the Cathedral.

Monastery entrance at Glendalough

The round tower is 100 feet high and its walls at the base are almost four feet thick; its purpose was to act as a strongroom for the monastery's valuables when the settlement was attacked. While the rest of the community fled to the safety of the mountains, a select few monks would enter the tower through the door twelve feet above the ground, draw up the ladder and lock the heavy door. Their pale frightened faces can be imagined peering out the little windows while Vikings rampaged below, no doubt attempting to burn or smoke them out before giving up in frustration and heading back for the sea.

Glendalough was first attacked by the Norsemen in 833, and their grandsons returned in 886 for another try. The early inhabitants of the newly founded city of Dublin raided the settlement in the tenth century and between these attacks and the numerous accidental fires which almost wiped out the settlement, the place has had an eventful history.

Near the Round Tower stands the remains of the Cathedral, the largest of the ruins at Glendalough. The antiquity of the place becomes more apparent when you realise that this building, although still called the Cathedral, ceased to be one when Glendalough was united with the Diocese of Dublin in 1214.

The walls inside are lined with memorial grave slabs whose dates range from the ninth to the nineteenth century. One commemorates a chieftain named Muirchertach Ua Cathalan who died in a local battle in 1151. See if you can spot the graveslab erected to a man who died in 1750 aged 106 years.

Downhill from the Cathedral is St Kevin's Church with the 'mini' round tower perched on its roof. This building is constructed from stone from foundation to roof, which probably explains why it is still intact after a thousand years. The graveyard here at Glendalough was not always as peaceful and picturesque as it is today. Up to the middle of the last century, St Kevin's Day on 3rd June was celebrated by a 'Pattern' that was as notorious for its faction fighting as it was renowned for its displays of devotion. Some years it took up to a hundred policemen to quell the rioting around the graveyard!

Follow the path downhill from St Kevin's Church and cross the river by the wooden bridge. Turning right, follow the pathway west past the Lower Lake through a lush green woodland of lichen covered beech, oak and holly trees.

Past the smaller Lower Lake, the Upper Lake presents a spectacular scene with the flanking mountains sweeping steeply down to the water. In the parkland around the eastern side of the lake are scattered more relics of ancient times including the ruins of two more churches, a circular stone fort, some weather-beaten stone crosses and the remains of a small circular stone building that may have been St Kevin's original hermitage.

A cave thirty feet above the lake level on the cliffside is known as St Kevin's bed, and although the saint may have spent time there, it was there long before he came to Glendalough and is thought to have originally been a Bronze Age tomb.

A herd of about sixty wild goats frequent the cliffs overlooking the Upper Lake. While there are a few herds of these animals in a number of inaccessible parts of the country, they are gradually dying out and may become extinct before long. The male goats grow spectacular long curled horns and the age of the animal can be calculated from the growth rings on the horns — but who would want to get that close!

In and around the cypress trees near the carpark you may have a chance of sighting the rarest and most colourful member of the crow family in Ireland — the jay. Often the jay is noticed by his raucous call, a harsh 'skaak'; he's a restless bird, always on the move from tree to tree, allowing only glimpses of his exotic azure, pink-buff, black and white markings and broad wings.

After crossing the bridge over the Lugduff brook, turn left and follow the footpath uphill. The brook flows noisily in a deep chasm hung down with mosses, ferns and lichens and a short distance uphill you will see Poll an Easa, a thundering waterfall which has, with the aid of grit, sand and time, polished the surface of the rock below into a smooth deep base.

After a steep climb the footpath meets a forest road; continue heading south through stately mature spruce trees interspersed with old twisted and gaunt oaks and birches. Turning left at a signpost that says 'Derrybawn Walk', cross the Lugduff stream again as the road loops back and go right at the next fork. The road climbs easily through mixed pine and larch trees until, about twenty minutes after passing Poll an Easa, it joins the Wicklow Way in a clearing overlooking the valley 400 feet below. If you carry on straight, the Wicklow Way takes you back to Laragh; a right turn follows the Way towards Mullacor and Glenmalure.

BALLINAFUNSHOGUE CIRCUIT
from Drumgoff and back

This is a route that takes in the main characteristics of the Glenmalure area, and can be completed in around four hours. There is some steep climbing and crossing of rough terrain involved and as Mullacor is quite remote this is not a suitable route for beginners.

Leaving Drumgoff Crossroads, follow the signpost for the Youth Hostel. In the gorse-strewn meadow on your left look out for a small memorial marking the graves of the two United Irishmen, killed here during the Rebellion of 1798. Beyond the meadow, the Avonbeg River meanders its way, providing as it follows the valley excellent picnic area and good swimming pools. It is also one of the few places along the Wicklow Way where otters can be seen.

A great granite boulder beside the road has tributes to the 1798 hero Michael Dwyer and Fiach McHugh O'Byrne carved on its east and west sides. O'Byrne was one of Ireland's foremost chieftains in the sixteenth century. Here deep in Wicklow he resisted English rule for many years, maintaining Irish customs, language and laws, and holding tenaciously on to his lands. He was a constant thorn in the side of the government, making frequent 'shopping trips' to the Pale of Dublin for cattle, arms and the odd hostage, after which he would disappear back into his mountain stronghold, where the English couldn't get at him. On one occasion, running low on shot for his stolen guns, O'Byrne visited Crumlin, south of Dublin, and took away the entire lead roof of the church!

In August 1580 Elizabeth I sent Lord Grey de Winton with a large force that included the poet Spenser and the young Sir Walter Raleigh, to eliminate O'Byrne. The English force entered Glenmalure at the western end and moved eastwards towards O'Byrne's settlement in the summer sun, clearly visible in their colourful uniforms to the Irish on the heights above, hidden in the boulders and bracken.

As the English force reached Ballyboy, the classic guerrilla tactic was used and somehow they were enticed uphill, relinquishing the safer level ground for the steep boulder-strewn incline. Soon the disciplined force became scattered and the Irish rose up from their hiding places and fell upon them. Slaughter ensued, while those still in the valley turned and fled; Lord Grey left his wardrobe and other belongings behind him in the panic. Eight hundred English are said to have died and it was many years before government forces again ventured into the mountains.

About twenty-five minutes after leaving the Glenmalure Hotel, Clohernagh Mountain (2,623 ft), one of Lugnaquillia's attendant foothills, comes into view over the scree-strewn wall of the far side of the valley. Just below Clohernagh the Carrowaystick waterfall can be seen thundering down to join the river.

Not far beyond the waterfall the road crosses a mound and passes through an area covered with heaps of whitish stone spoil. This is what remains of a busy lead mining industry that was carried on in Glenmalure 150 years ago. Numerous adits or tunnels were carved into the valley sides, (the spillage of waste from one can be seen above to the right here) and during the 1830s they were producing 400 tons of lead ore per year. Today if you look for a piece of white quartz with grey shadows in it, and use a large rock to break it open, you will be rewarded with the discovery of diamond-like lustrous silver grey crystals of gelena, or lead ore. With the exception of the ruins across the river, the mine buildings have now disappeared to contribute to field walls in the valley.

Not far beyond the entrance to Ballinafunshogue Wood, where there is an idyllic picnic spot near a waterfall, the western edge of the wood is reached, a little over an hour after leaving Drumgoff crossroads. Turn uphill and climb the steep slope parallel to the trees; this is very heavy going at first, but the gradient eases considerably after about twenty minutes. Pause frequently to regain your breath and enjoy the ever changing and spectacular views unfolding below and spare a thought for those poor soldiers who tried to fight their way uphill near here in 1580.

The forestry roads come to the edge of the trees on the way up; cross a stile onto the second one and after a few minutes watch for a break in the trees going uphill, with a Wicklow Way pointer. Turn up this break and exit onto the open mountain below Mullacor about fifteen minutes after crossing the stile.

Follow the Wicklow Way pointers left and then right onto a track going north, marked with posts. When the posts turn left towards the flat-topped Turlough Hill, turn right uphill beside the ploughed ground.

After a steep climb the top of Mullacor (described on pages 49-50), is reached about twenty minutes after leaving the trees. Head for a couple of old fence posts visible ahead and when the fence divides follow the one going right. Take care with your footing as you descend steeply down the east side of Mullacor; there are frequent holes in the ground and rusted barbed wire from the old fence to be watched for.

Now the valley of Ballybraid opens up below, with the partly harvested Ballinafunshogue Wood on the right and the treeless expanse of Cullentragh Mountain on the left. The lower of the two forestry roads running eastwards along Ballinafunshogue and Ballyboy is your route back to Drumgoff. At the north west corner of the harvested wood, cross to the other side of the fence and continue downhill, crossing the barbed-wire fence carefully to reach the top of the forestry road about fifteen minutes after leaving the summit.

At a fork in the road, turn sharp left and continue downhill. When you reach the bottom of the long straight, go sharp left at the fork and descend to the valley floor, taking the left turn at the next junction and crossing the river. Turning right at the next junction, the public road is reached in a few minutes; keeping on downhill, Drumgoff Crossroads is about fifteen minutes away.